HOUSE OF MANY ROOMS

selected poems

nancy corbett

© Nancy Corbett 2024

All rights reserved. Except for appropriate use in a book review, no part of this publication may be reproduced, stored in a retrieval system, or transmitted in any form or by any means, without the prior permission of the publisher, or in the case of photocopying or reprographic copying, a licence from the Copyright Agency of Australia.

TITLE: HOUSE OF MANY ROOMS / NANCY CORBETT

ISBN 978-0-6480821-2-5

Cover Image by Bruce Penn
Title: "Sunrise in the Wardrobe"
(coloured pencil drawing on A4 bamboo paper)

Walleah Press
South Launceston
Tasmania, Australia 7249

www.walleahpress.com.au
ralph.wessman@walleahpress.com.au

HOUSE OF MANY ROOMS

*Finding the words
is another step
in learning to see.*
Robin Wall Kimmerer

Drawing by Sonja Hindrum

I was told in a university class that good poetry is written by the young, and good novels by the more mature. I've often puzzled over this.

Is it that poetry needs passion, and old people don't have it? And that novels need wisdom, and young people don't have it?

I don't think age has anything to do with either passion or wisdom. Passion is experienced and wisdom acquired by young and old alike – or not.

I hope you find passion, wisdom and a few smiles in *House of Many Rooms.*

CONTENTS

ONE: WATER IS ALL..................................... 7
IKITTIBANA... 9
MY LIFE IS A HOUSE WITH MANY ROOMS.............. 11
TIME/WATER... 13
TREES... 15
WHEN ALL THIS IS OVER.................................. 17
AT FATEHPUR SIKRI....................................... 19
APPLE... 21

TWO: WHERE WE ARE.................................. 23
ACCEPT/EXCEPT... 25
ANIMALS... 27
BEHIND CLOSED DOORS.................................. 29
THOUGHTS ON SUNDAY................................... 31
BOTANY BAY.. 33

THREE: DON'T GET ME STARTED.................... 35
ROWING TEAM ON THE YARRA.......................... 37
RIGHT NOW.. 39
ESCAPE VACATION.. 41
WHEREAS:... 43
BRITISH COLUMBIA JULY................................ 45

FOUR: SWING MUSIC...	47
SON..	49
ANSWERS..	51
KYRIELLE...	53
SWING..	55
ANOTHER ADDICTION POEM..	57
STUBBORN...	59
FIVE: IT STILL MATTERS..	*61*
AGING..	*61*
WHAT WE DO...	63
AUBADE IN SUMMER..	65
something I said..	67
TEAPOT...	69
SIX: GOTTA BE ME...	*71*
CANADIAN HAIKU..	*71*
PRIME TIME..	73
GOTTA BE ME..	75
MAX..	77
CHILLY POEM..	79
THE ARROGANT FROG...	81

ONE: WATER IS ALL

IKITTIBANA

Henry loved things Japanese;
Haiku with chips, kimono sleeves,
Cranes on water, mist on bridges,
Shrines on mountains, pines on ridges.

He had two cats, one white, one black,
One was Basho, one was Jack.
He trained them in the art of space:
Ikittibana, feline grace.

MY LIFE IS A HOUSE WITH MANY ROOMS

At the foundation, two babies;
one is sleeping sweetly; warm, dry & loved
& one is screaming, screaming.

On the first floor are all the trees and animals,
the rivers & the stars, the ocean shore,
the birds & frogs & praying mantises;
& the room with picture books & games,
& the room filled with music,
& the hallway with a bicycle, ice skates & running shoes.

The next floor is an enormous library
containing every book I've ever read,
(with space for all the ones I've yet to read);
there's a desk in this room too,
& on the desk, a journal & a pen.
a tabby cat is sleeping on the chair.

The kitchen on the floor above
is bright and welcoming;
there's a fireplace, a basket for the dog,
and room for all my friends around the wooden table
to talk & laugh with me
while we prepare our favourite food.
also here are many private rooms
for friends who come to stay.

One floor up is my boudoir,
with fine soft sheets & radiance of candles;
perfumes, toys for lovers, lingerie,
one big bowl of perfect cherries,
two crystal glasses, a flask of sparkling water,
& a bath just big enough for two.

The floor above, two studios.
one for writing,
& no one enters here except for me.
the second's full of paints, beads, shells & stones,
glue & paper, cloth & every tool I need
for making things.

The smallest room is at the very top.
its walls are glass & it's completely bare,
the sky above its only ornament.
here my spirit finds a resting place
in utter stillness.

My house is as big as the world,
& as small as a handful of brain cells.

My house is a life with many rooms.
My life is a house with many rooms.

TIME/WATER

Time flows
wearing us away
like water
wearing us away   and
bearing us away   and
wearing us smooth

Time
mistress of all the world
empress of elements
carrying all before it
creating all
destroying all
recreating and
always moving   and
never
stops

We float in time
and we are mostly water
we are sea
we are rivers of life
moving on dry land
for a little time
standing in air
for a little time
before returning
to the endless time
the mother sea

Here
for a little time
the well fills   and
water flows   and
time slows

TREES

the life of trees
is the life of air
and earth

the life of trees
is a clock
that measures centuries

the life of trees
makes homes for countless lives
beavers, beetles, birds

the life of trees
blesses the sky
and reaches deep

embracing stones
and sheltering
innumerable hidden beings

the life of trees
is a Trinity

understory
overstory
and the long green narrative of life.

WHEN ALL THIS IS OVER

when all this is over
I mean to keep the spaces
and the silence
which I did not welcome
but learned to value
came to love.

I mean to stop putting off
the things I was too busy for
when, too preoccupied with others
and needing to read too many books
days, weeks, months and years
(my life)
passed away.

Too fast, too fast.

I want to see with eyes
made clear by solitude
I want to turn from noise
to sounds of wind, of water
reading only poems
and prose that reads like poem
words slipping smooth
strong and beautiful
as stones in mountain streams.

AT FATEHPUR SIKRI

Emperor Akbar
King of the Mughals
built a great city
the colour of roses
City of Victory
larger than London.

Supreme work of art
from a great civilisation
palaces, temples
courtyards and pillars
all from one vision
all of red sandstone.

City of Victory
empty, deserted
not enough water.

Power is nothing
empire is nothing

Water is all.

APPLE

This apple is. It just . . . is.

Small, tart, streaked with red and gold.
Pucker at the pointy end
a memory of blossom.

Inside, its seeds
hold blueprints for an orchard.
Can seeds imagine
their massive possibilities?
And what of us?
Born of two microscopic cells
smaller than apple seeds
Can we?

Apple.
Christian symbol of the Fall of Man
through Woman, snake and rosy, tempting fruit.

Really?

More an icon of salvation,
generation, plenty, pleasure;
if symbol is, at all.

The apple is. It just . . . is.

TWO: WHERE WE ARE

*fisherman
waiting
still as stone*

*reflection
wavering
among ripples*

ACCEPT/EXCEPT

trying to accept
life on life's terms
except
how can I
accept
war, pestilence, fire and flood?
those apocalyptic horsemen
riding roughshod
over the desperate earth?

how can I accept
when accepting
may mean apathy
except if purpose rises
giving birth to action
creating change?

too often, overwhelmed
by the depths and breadth
of what's needed
I feel useless
except when writing

though I accept
that writing changes nothing
except when I remember
that's not true

kudos to
old Percy Shelley
who said that
poets are
the unacknowledged legislators
of the world

for words have often
led the way
moved the people
yes
changed the world.

ANIMALS

some are mysterious
others have transparent hearts

some go to any length to avoid us
others, any length to come along

the ones we're drawn to
reveal more about us
than them
more about our character
than theirs

and we have too much power
in these relationships
unless we're kind
and wise

wisdom and kindness
not universal qualities
in human animals

BEHIND CLOSED DOORS

John and Yoko
in Annie Leibowitz's famous photo
cover of Rolling Stone
January 22 1981

most men I know
hate it

a woman clothed and calm,
self-contained
a naked, needy man
nude, hairless, no big muscles

he looks weak and
she looks strong

if he were clothed
and she was naked
we'd scarcely notice

it might just be
an ad for perfume
or shoes or whisky
it would be *normal*
perfectly normal

but real, normal men
cling to their woman sometimes
vulnerable, childlike

but only in secret
behind closed doors

how brave of John and Yoko.

6 hours later, John was dead.

Perhaps there's no connection.

THOUGHTS ON SUNDAY

stars and rocks and shells
deeps of oceans
heights of mountains
spread of an old oak

a wall of books
kept and never lost
over a long lifetime
of loving books
and many, many moves

constancy of sunrise
comfort of the night
infinity of space
race of change
strength of love

we're new here
and like young children
our greed and curiosity
have made the place a mess

and I wonder if
we're almost old enough
to put things back
where they belong

BOTANY BAY

the world sailed into Botany Bay
a moment or two ago
trailing its chain of consequences.

we're still unsure
of where we are
and who we are
and learning it is painful.

What have we done?
And what can be undone?

We need to see, and care
before we can belong.

All their stories
are made of air and singing
their memories and knowledge
still live
in living people

the silver ashes
of all their fires
are still beneath our feet.

THREE: DON'T GET ME STARTED

ROWING TEAM ON THE YARRA

the river is precious metal
beaten bronze
silver
fading to rose

they row in silence
dip and lift
dip and lift

they become one thing
centred
one being   with six long arms
pulling itself smoothly
across the glittered surface

current flows beneath
they fly above its pull
swift, light
lift, bright
sprays of sparkle
no talk
no laughter

just for this moment
they slip from separateness
to be part of the river's life

RIGHT NOW

Human
humane
humanity

homo sapiens
not so much
homo ludens
not enough

we're living the vida loca
the anthropocene
the manmade world

eating the earth
the sea
the sky

gobbling it like chips
risking it like Sportsbets
wrapping it all in plastic

faster, faster, faster
you can eat it faster
if you try
more, more, more
you can get more
if you try

seven billion of us
and a car for everyone

a dozen screens
for every one of
our 14 billion eyes
shoes for every one of
our 14 billion feet

highrise homes
carved into tiny rooms
without windows
without kitchens
you can call the Uber

how to escape?
where to escape?
from our own
endless needs
and wants and whims

pockets of sanity remain
here and there
in human hearts
here and there
in human minds
here and there
in fugitive groves of trees
in remnants of wildness

one in three great rivers
still flows free
a few animals
still find instinctive ways
between our rubbish dumps

and there are stars at night
between the satellites
and blinking lights of planes
full of tourists and business people
going faster
to eat more of the world

before
it's
all

gone

ESCAPE VACATION

escape and
run away and
find a new landscape
pay a lot of money
see some nature
use a lot of airplane fuel
to escape your anxiety
about the environmental crisis

have a meal or three
on the airplane
it's hygienic
you might break a nail
but you won't get sick
it's vacuumsealed
in plastic
against all living things

fly to somewhere
less civilised
more natural
look at the trees
look at the water
look at the people
pity their poverty
admire their simpler lives
think for a moment
how good it would be
to live a simple life
then walk away

fly home
use lots of airplane fuel
eat hygienic snacks
tightwrapped in plastic

show the photos on your phone
to all your friends
tell them
how nice it was
how good it was
to visit a place
unspoiled by tourists
the people there are poor
and need the money you spend
(though most of it went to Qantas
where the CEO got 9 million a year)
and airplane gas is expensive
especially with all the new wars

Don't get me started.
Oh, wait; I already did.

WHEREAS:

Whereas people have traditionally
given names to everything
and divided mammals into **us,** humans,
and **them**, dumb animals

and whereas dumb means
unable to speak
and/or (colloquially, mistakenly) stupid

and whereas every animal I've ever spoken to
especially dogs
especially cats
especially horses
has spoken back quite clearly

and not just mammals
but birds and frogs
and even bumblebees

and whereas humans seem to need
(and think they have the right)
to define all other things

and assign specific names
to other sentient beings
without even asking

and whereas lots of humans
act pretty dumb
(as in stupid)

and whereas I'm fairly sure
all animals know who and what they are
without needing
an assigned external name

and whereas I'm almost certain
all cats have secret names
known only to themselves

and all dogs and horses
elephants, panthers
mountain goats and mice
know who they are
and are not dumb at all

therefore: let it be resolved
to practise some humility;

when talking to non-humans,
speak gently,
and listen with respect.

BRITISH COLUMBIA JULY

summer roadside
dusty blue chicory
white vetch and toadflax
old names still there
from distant childhood

in a meadow, a fat pony
up to her belly
in white daisies

distant mountains keep the peace

expatriate now
aware of the critic
in my head
commenting
on every goddamn RV
passing by

here in the first world
in summer
life gets simple

all you need is
a motorhome
a 4-wheel drive
a boat
a tv
sound system
roof racks
couple of motorbikes
mountain bike
and you're all set
off you go
to play

my god what a great summer day it is
and here's me carping at it all
while I walk along the road
looking for some place to spend money
a Baskin Robbins
or a Lucky Dollar
just like everybody else

at least I have
enough sense
to laugh at myself.

FOUR: SWING MUSIC

*Seed is both
container and content;
memory
and map of what's to come.*

Bed No _____ Room No _301_

Name _Babe Knowlton_

Date of Birth _July 28/60_ Time _8:15_ a.m.

Birth Weight _6_ lbs _3_ oz. Length _____ in.

Doctor _Skye_

SON

I grew you in my body
birthed   you
named   you
Christopher
held you four short days
signed their papers
before you disappeared
into your unknown life.

the ones who said
they knew better
advised me to forget   you
to pretend   you
never happened

didn't tell me
how, exactly,
do I do that?

part of my mind forgot
but not my body
and every year
on your (forgotten) birth day
chaos danced into my life
bright-eyed
and looking for trouble.

until I remembered
to remember   you
and never forgot   you
again.

ANSWERS

I don't know the question

and

I've been looking in the wrong places
looking in the wrong eyes
telling lies

trying too hard
burning too bright
drinking too much
falling too fast

stopping at last

frightened of stopping
what if I die?

frightened of dying
what if I stop?

KYRIELLE

The birds are silent in the air
I want to speak but do not dare;
The clouds are weaving wisps of song,
This day is very very long.

The sun may rise, the sun will set
I know a truth I must forget;
The darkness muffles every song,
This day is very very long.

You spoke although I heard no words
I searched the air but found no birds;
I longed to hear one silvery song,
This day is very very long.

SWING

My brother and his lady love to dance
they love that old time swing music and
I'm watching as he twirls her out and back
her flared skirt swinging round her
they're both smiling; they're loving it
and loving themselves, dancing, quick then slow
across the polished floor, they can't sit down
not with that music playing, not while
her skirt keeps swinging and the band keeps playing
that music; that good old rhythmic swing.

It made me remember those long afternoons
Mum working at the hospital, me too young for school
I'm with my dad in his workshop;
smells of oil and wood
dusty light through small high windows
the black Lab, Timmy, asleep under the bench
me with some scraps of wood, some jars of odds and ends
nails and bolts and screws, and the old bakelite radio
with the woven fabric front and the big band music
Tommy Dorsey and Glen Miller, Guy Lombardo
swing music swinging and my dad whistling in tune.

ANOTHER ADDICTION POEM

I won't forget
and don't want to
the way you looked last night
when you didn't know
I saw you;

head in your arms,
a statue of despair,
overwhelmed,
defeated.

A powerful person
powerless;
your strength
diminished by my weakness.

A part of what I am
has hurt you;
taught you things
you didn't want to know
and
things I didn't want to know
and
things I didn't want you to know.

I have to find my strength
and give yours back.

STUBBORN

Hanging on, hanging in
I can't give up, I can't give in.

My God but you're a stubborn woman
you said.

(there was a time when you admired that;
a time you called it strength.)

You're hard, you said.

Hard?

Perhaps I am
and if I am
let me be hard like a seed.

That makes sense.

Seeds are hard
to shield the life
inside enfolded
encasing as they do
the wisdom
of a million generations
holding as they do
minute, precise blueprints for trees
containing as they do
chemistry labs
for making beans and banksias
pumpkins and puffballs.

Seed is both
container and content;
memory
and map of what's to come.

So let me be
stubborn as a seed
and, like a seed
unable to be other
than I am.

FIVE: IT STILL MATTERS

AGING

*The lengthening list of losses,
the kinder eye,
the longer wait to judge;*

*but still unable not to see
our stubborn, fierce stupidity.*

WHAT WE DO

small as we are
in this unbounded universe
it still matters
what we think
and
what we do

it's a terrible thought
a wonderful thought
because the choice is ours
at every moment
we have to watch our mind
our step
our behaviour
and its consequences

learning, seeing, judging,
charting the many paths
that lead to self
and selflessness

surely I am too small
to make a difference?
surely I can live
(and die)
without affecting anything?

but everything is part of everything
nothing is meaningless

it's glorious
it's tragic
it's beyond our comprehension
it seems beyond our strength

but small as we are
it matters
what we think
and
what we do.

AUBADE IN SUMMER

First, the plovers.
Vanellus Miles;

their penetrating cry
shivers the lightening dark
just as first lightlines
brush golden edges
on the dark silk curtains
of the eastern sky.

A long day is beginning.
A hard day is beginning.

In all its hours
I hope to hold
this edge of gold
and the plover's cry.

something I said

something I said
some way I said it
closed you like a fist
against me.

you went somewhere
I couldn't follow;
left no doors open,
no crack of light
to show where you might be.

shut
tight as a stone
you lay there.

when I spoke,
no answer.
when I touched you,
every cell said NO
to me.

that was
the loudest silence
I ever heard.

TEAPOT

You said you didn't like her
that's what you said
but you admired her as an artist
that's what you said
the fine engraving
the gold and silver leaf
the delicate embossing
the semiprecious gems
so opulent and enticing.

You bought a piece
a silver teapot
it was a gift for me
that's what you said
perhaps you were afraid
to tell me what it cost
to say how much you'd given her.

I'm no detective.
I didn't have to be
to notice the perfume
when I kissed you.
I don't wear perfume.

The airplane is ready for boarding.
I've wrapped the teapot
to give to my sister.
I hold it in both hands
and kiss you goodbye.

Goodbye.

SIX: GOTTA BE ME

CANADIAN HAIKU

Short night is ending;
as stars melt into dawn light
the loon calls and calls.

PRIME TIME

We're told that desire belongs to the young
that its sharpness is blunted by time;
but that is a lie
told by those who don't know
the pleasure of love in their prime.

I will not pretend that new isn't nice
or deny the attraction of youth;
but older is golden,
it's sweeter and slower,
and friendlier; that is the truth.

We both know our bodies better these days
we're lovers and partners and friends;
now I come much faster
while he comes much slower
and both of us reach happy ends.

We enjoy it most in the morning
there's no need to wait until night;
we don't have to rush
to get to a job
there's time to do everything right.

I don't miss making love on the table
or squashed against the bark of a tree;
no, delights in the doona
sensual sessions in spas
and bliss in our bed, for me.

GOTTA BE ME

When I was young, I fell in love the way we usually do
He was absolutely gorgeous and a drummer in a band;
I wanted him forever but he told me, shooting through;
I gotta be me, I gotta be free, you just don't understand.

I married someone different, a decent sort of bloke
We had the rings, we had the kids, we had the future planned;
But he said as he was leaving me, alone and sad and broke;
I gotta be me, I gotta be free, you just don't understand.

One kid grew up and stole my car, the other was a lout
Victims of the zeitgeist and some sort of feral gland;
And what did they both say to me the day they both moved out?
I gotta be me, I gotta be free, you just don't understand.

But one by one they each came back from where they each had been
I was kind of glad to see them, but on the other hand,
I told them they could visit but they couldn't move back in;
I gotta be me, I gotta be free, I'm sure they understand.

MAX

I'm going to tell you a story
and everything in it is facts;
in the loft of a barn on Windover's farm
lives the ghost of a goose named Max.

Mad Max was a terror when he was alive
we tried to avoid him, in vain;
as we waited in fear for the school bus
Max found us again and again.

Max was big, he was bad, and a bully
a blow from his wings broke your arm;
he hissed like a steam train, he ran like a racer
his malevolent eye promised harm.

I don't know who finally killed him
there were several who wanted him gone;
no one owned up but we all felt relief
that the murderous deed had been done.

But he isn't *quite* gone, in the loft of the barn
there's a feeling of doom to this day;
too evil to die, his spirit hangs on
as a horrible hiss in the hay.

CHILLY POEM

Oh Canada, oh Canada
my northern birthplace dear
much of it is wild
and its winters are severe.

In wintertime it freezes hard
there's frost and ice and snow
there's howling winds and temperatures
of 20 degrees below.

So down I came to Sydney
expecting winters fine
for sitting in the sunlight
in my garden, drinking wine.

Our house was tall, our house was old
and in all its generous space
there was one tiny 2-bar heater
to warm the bloody place.

The windows let the cold in
there was damp on every wall
and in the night the chilly wind
blew along the hall.

It was chilly in the bedroom
it was chilly in the loo
it was chilly everybloodywhere
and nothing we could do.

It was frigid in the kitchen
it was freezing in the lounge
we took to wearing blankets
or whatever we could scrounge.

Our faces froze, our hands were blue
we spent most days in bed
and I hated meeting Aussies
because they always said

From Canada? You must be glad
To get away from there
Where winters are horrendous
And much too cold to bear.

But no, my friend, it's not like that
the houses there are *heated*;
you don't need coats and gloves inside
the winter cold's defeated.

Don't get me wrong, I love it here
an Aussie proud I stand;
but I've **never** been as cold as that
first winter in the great south land.

THE ARROGANT FROG

Arrogant? I don't think so.
I do have self esteem;
and it's true that some have called me
the handsomest frog in the stream.

But I am essentially humble
living quietly here in the bog;
I swim, I sleep, I make *l'amour*
like every other frog.

It's true my voice is deep and pure
my skin is emerald green;
I admit my jumps are *magnifique*
and the lady frogs are keen.

But when you call me arrogant
I do not like your tone;
I may be a very superior frog
but arrogant? *Moi? Mais non!*

www.ingramcontent.com/pod-product-compliance
Lightning Source LLC
Chambersburg PA
CBHW022021290426
44109CB00015B/1259